A LASTING EFFECT

Reflections on Music and Medicine

Bryan Sisk

Cover design by Bryan Sisk
Cover was created with the help of Jim Lang, Justin Johnson, and Dairoll Medrano.

ISBN-13: 978-1461025610
ISBN-10: 1461025613

Printed in the United States of America.

First Edition

To my wife, for always loving me and supporting my crazy ideas.

To the children in this book, who became my teachers and made my world a little bigger over the last three years.

CONTENTS:

take a guitar
add fingers &
a heart
pour on
study & learning
test it thru
the pediatrics ward
to jump start
forgetfulness &
laughter &
you have git man sisk
healing w/song

~jim lang

Introduction

Epilepsy, cancer, sickle cell anemia, heart failure. For three years during medical school, I had the amazing privilege to play guitar and sing songs with kids at the Cleveland Clinic Children's Hospital who suffered from these types of diseases. While I provided a diversion for these kids, a distraction from the mundane and sterile nature of any hospital, they taught me about resilience, love, faith and hope. These families allowed me into their lives during the scariest and most vulnerable moments they had ever experienced... and all I had to give in return were a few songs.

This book is a compilation and distillation of all my experiences with these children and the lessons they taught me. The stories contained within this book are filled with laughter and tears, both mine and the families'. But these stories also show the uncanny ability of children to understand and hold onto the most important things in life. Unburdened by years of stress and indoctrination into adulthood, these kids have an inherent ability to cut through the distractions that muddy up adult life. Hopefully, these stories will help the reader to return, at least momentarily, to the innocent mindset of a child.

Lastly, I would like to say that this book is not about me; this book is about the children that welcomed me into their lives, and it is about the power we all have to make positive changes in the world, regardless of the scale. While volunteering at the Children's Hospital, if I met a child who was interested in learning to play guitar, I always offered encouragement. Then I followed by saying, "Well, if you learn to play guitar, then you can come back in ten years and do what I am doing at the hospital. Wouldn't it be great to be able to play music for sick kids?" Now I offer the same challenge to you, the reader. After finishing this book, if you feel any impulse to seek out opportunities to help others in your own unique way, I implore you to follow your heart. You may be amazed by the outcome.

Guitar Lessons

I always began by introducing myself and explaining the two rules: "My name is Bryan. I'm a medical student, and I play guitar in the hospital every week. I would love to play some music for you, but there are two rules: Number one – I will play as long as you want me to; and number two – you can laugh at me if I mess up!" This always seemed to draw a smile from the patient. It must have been easier to smile when a stranger entered their hospital room with a guitar instead of a white coat or scrubs. There was no fear of an ulterior motive: no needles, no blood draws, no EEG leads, no chemotherapy, no procedures. On Monday afternoons, I set aside my title of medical student and assumed my role as "volunteer musical services," a title I had invented for myself. During those two or three hours each week, I strolled through the inpatient and outpatient pediatric departments of the hospital with my guitar in hand and played music for sick kids. After three years of encounters with these young patients, I have collected a full spectrum of profound experiences and memories.

One particular patient continues to stand out in my mind. I will call her "Laney." When we first met, it was only my third week volunteering at the hospital. I was still learning how to interact with these young patients, trying to determine my role as I shifted between medical student and musician. Before I went to visit Laney's room, her doctor shared her story with me. She was a 12-year-old girl who had previously been a musician and an actress. Her mother had told me stories of her playing violin, acting in musicals, and taking voice lessons. She loved to perform, no matter the venue. But this all changed. The first time I visited her, she was three days post-op following surgical removal of a brain tumor. Although the surgeon had carefully excised the mass, the cancer had already damaged the surrounding tissue. The disease and the treatment had combined to leave Laney completely debilitated: unable to move, unable to talk.

My eyes pored over the sad sight in front of me when I entered her room. She was lying on her back in the hospital bed with a loose gown draped over her skinny body. Her chest gently raised and lowered as she breathed, hardly noticeable under her gown and blanket. Her left forearm was pierced

4

by an IV line, with medications and fluids slowly entering her vein from the bag hanging at her bedside. Her bald head was perfectly smooth except for a C-shaped incision on the right side just above her ear, where the surgeon had passed through Laney's skull into her brain. Now, the skin was tightly sewn with thick black sutures, each stitch dimpling the surrounding skin. A solitary drop of blood hung from the last stitch.

Her eyes stared intensely into mine as I introduced myself. I masked my anxiety with a smile and asked if Laney wanted to hear any music. Her mother turned to her and said, "Now, sweetie, tell Bryan if you want to hear some music." With great effort, she turned her left hand into the "thumbs up" position. This was the only extremity that she could move, her only means of communication with the outside world. As I began to strum the guitar and sing, I noticed a change in Laney's face; she could smile too – at least, with the left side of her mouth. After finishing the first song, I asked if they wanted to hear another. Laney gave another unsteady "thumbs up." Forty-five minutes and several more "thumbs ups" later, we had played through my entire stack of music. After giving my farewell, I left the room burdened with conflicting emotions. I was glad to have consoled a distressed young girl, but I was also saddened by the belief that she would never recover from her current condition.

Two weeks passed before I next saw Laney. At first sight, I noticed a difference in her. Her body had assumed a more natural, relaxed posture in the bed, and she was smiling from both sides of her mouth. She was also able to lift her arm completely off of the bed to wave hello to me when I entered the room. The neurons in her brain were dutifully working to reconnect, attempting to salvage some facet of normalcy. Given this improvement, I decided to challenge her. I placed a maraca in her hand and asked her to shake while I played the guitar. Song after song, her stiff arm weaved in and out of rhythm with our music. Yet again, we played through all of my songs. As I stood up to leave and walked towards the door, I heard a high-pitched voice weakly say "Thank you." After speaking these words, she deflated into the bed. This simple task had drained all of her energy.

Laney continued to progress over the next few weeks, and she was eventually transferred to a rehabilitation center and subsequently sent home. At that point, I was not sure if I would ever see her or her mother again, but nearly three months later we were reunited. Fortunately, her outpatient visits were scheduled during the time that I played guitar, allowing me to follow Laney on a weekly basis for several more months. When we had our first reunion, I was amazed by her progress. She was talking and she could stand with the help of leg braces. Although she was still fairly debilitated, she and her mother were in the process of redefining normal. Success was a matter of outlook, and we all saw the success in Laney's story.

Following the usual pattern, I asked if she wanted to hear any music, knowing she would say yes. The first song was one that I had played for her every week when she was paralyzed in her hospital bed. As I began to sing, I noticed another voice accompanying me. With her eyes closed, Laney was singing the song with me. After all the weeks of playing and singing to her paralyzed body, she had memorized the words to the song. Although her body could not move, her active mind was always there with me, absorbing and recording the words. Yet again, she had surpassed my preconceived expectations.

Over the course of the next several months, we continued our weekly visits. Her speech continually improved and she eventually began to walk with the assistance of a modified walker. Her prognosis continued to improve as well. The chemotherapy was working and there was no sign of cancer. With each new scan, the physicians felt more and more confident that she was "cured," the magical word that oncologists use only with great caution.

Finally, the day came when Laney received her last infusion of chemotherapy. After this last treatment, it was unlikely that we would have any future music sessions. Our final guitar session was filled with as many emotions as our first. Over the year that we knew each other, I had grown quite attached to this young girl and her resilient spirit. I realized how much I would miss our guitar sessions together, but I was also overjoyed to see her return to the life of a teenage girl. She had suffered enough.

We played through our usual songs and talked about their hopes and plans for the upcoming year: musicals, vacations, school. Eventually, I gave her my final farewell and received hugs from both mother and daughter before walking out of the room. My experience with Laney had come to a conclusion; it was time for each of us to start new stories. After leaving her room, I knocked on the next patient's door. It was a young boy whom I had never met, so I introduced myself. "My name is Bryan. I am a medical student, and I play guitar on Mondays. I would love to play some music for you, but there are two rules…"

Two Different Worlds

I switched from white coat to guitar
And walked down the hall
A young girl with shaved head
Looked confused as she said
"I remember you
You were a doctor last week
You came into that room
In a white coat to see me"
I smile, nod and try to explain
I live in two different worlds
Depending on the day

Homemade Riffs

I see him through the doorway
Eighteen years old
In simple clothes
Homemade at first glance
His mother is right beside
Her dress a simple blue,
A bonnet covering her
Bun of hair
They speak to each other
In Pennsylvania Dutch
The modified German
Of the Mennonites
He came to fight the cancer
That's eating his marrow
And choking his blood
The nurse said there's
Not much time left
The cancer won't budge
Despite the worst drugs

I stand by the door
With a guitar in my hands

Not sure if I should knock,
Not sure if the Amish like music,
Not sure if they like *my* music
I break through
This self-imposed taboo
And enter the room

I say hello and
Tell them my role
"I'm a med student by day
But I play at the hospital
During my breaks"
With a slight smile on his face
The patient tells me that
He's teaching himself to play
I offer him the guitar and a pick
And wait for him to begin

His fingers run up and down
The length of the neck
Hammering the strings while
The other hand furiously picks
To create a lick
The music is like nothing
I have ever heard
Without a radio in his home
His musical style was
All his own

He invented riffs that
Told a story only he could tell
His story
A story of life seen through
His unique view
A story of death creeping
Too close, too soon

A Lasting Effect

My eyes immediately focused on the bandaged stump and the empty space where his leg used to be. The nurse had warned me before I entered the room, but I was still jolted by the sight. The surgeons had amputated his leg just two days before, below the knee. This was the last resort, a life-saving measure. How must it feel to be seventeen years old with only one leg? I forced my gaze away from his wound and met his eyes. They were swollen and tired, probably a combination of pain, medications, and the stress of starting a new life feeling less than whole. I tried to bury my sadness while conjuring a soft smile.

"Hi. My name is Bryan. I'm a medical student, but I play music at the hospital every week. Would you like to hear any songs?" He nodded his head slightly forward in assent. I placed my stack of worn and wrinkled song sheets in his hand, and while he was browsing through the selection, his mother said, "Well, you know *he* plays guitar, too." Warm maternal pride filled her eyes.

"That's great. How long have you been playing?" I asked him.

"Since I was ten," he responded with a scratchy voice.

"Wow, seven years. I've only been playing since my last year of college—about four years." I began to feel insecure about playing for a musician with more experience than I had. "Why don't you play something first?" I offered. He weakly nodded his head again. His forearms were pocked with multiple IV lines, each connected to a hanging bag, and his chest had a painful incision that was covered with thick gauze and medical tape. We snaked my guitar through the gauntlet of medical paraphernalia and carefully rested it on his stomach. He winced as he tried to reposition himself in the bed in search of a comfortable position.

Once he was settled, he began to pick a rhythm on the guitar. He played slowly and deliberately, trying to fight through the medication haze, persistently coaxing his fingers to follow orders. After a few stumbles, a tune emerged and danced around the room. Then in the midst of his song, he winced harshly through gritted teeth and suddenly stopped playing. His ailing body had sent his brain a reminder of his condition; he could no longer play through his pain. With a frustrated gasp, he surrendered the guitar.

As I returned the guitar to my shoulders, he began to search again through the stack of papers for a familiar song. He looked over my entire catalog before making his first selection. It was one of the most difficult songs I knew how to play. Like a true guitarist, he wanted to test my skills. I took a deep breath and began the song. His eyes were fixed on my fingers as they plucked and strummed, jumped from fret to fret, hammered-on and pulled-off, bent the strings with bluesy inflection. He seemed to critique every move and every note. His face was painted with intent pleasure.

We played through several songs over the next half hour, each just as difficult. While I played, his eyes were full of life, no longer obscured by pain or worries. He had transcended his problems and found peace in a musical refuge. The music had provided shelter from his stormy life. As the final note faded, reality began to seep back into the room. His eyes lost their depth and forgotten pains quickly registered. Once again, he was a seventeen-year-old boy in a hospital with one leg and several scars.

As I watched his painful transformation, I was sadly reminded that every song must end. My guitar could not undo the harms that he had suffered, and the relief I offered was merely a momentary diversion. My guitar was not a panacea. Regardless, I was convinced that something more than a diversion had taken place. I believed that, in some way, our music would live on beyond the end of that last song. Although he was reeling in pain at that moment, perhaps he felt a trifle less pain because of our music. And later that night when he was lying alone in the hospital bed, perhaps he felt a little less lonely because of my visit. And someday ahead when the memories of his suffering have slowly subsided, perhaps he might be reminded of the songs that made him smile on the worst day of his life. And maybe he will smile again and pick up his guitar.

<u>A Birthday Wish</u>

You made it one year
Here's your reward
Recovering from surgery
That stole part of your brain
What else it stole
Only time will tell
All your family can do
Is hope and pray

The swelling has forced
Your eyes tightly shut
Your mouth a mere dimple
In mountains of cheeks
Your mother rocks you sweetly
In her warm embrace
Leans in and kisses
Your gauze forehead
Says it's your first birthday
Early next week
"Could you sing Happy Birthday?
It would mean a great deal"

I gladly oblige
And as we begin
You force your eyes open
And take me in
We all are surprised
By this sudden glance
You've not opened your eyes
Since surgery began
I see the tears stream
Down your mother's cheeks
And reach to wipe
My own damp eyes
Not sure if I should
Let the tears run free
Or bury them deep
In stoic routine

These times must be trying
I can hardly guess
How your family must feel
As they watch your fight
If it's any consolation
I'd be happy to give
My next birthday wishes
To you instead

I wish good surprises
Will continue to come

And your future is normal
This disease overcome
I wish you run and play
And scrape your knees
While growing in mischief
And curiosity
I wish you make friends
And tease the boys
Pass from cooties to crushes
And fall in love
I wish you happiness
In whatever you do
And may you live a life
That uniquely suits you
I wish you many birthday cakes
Over the years
And I wish you birthday candles
That refuse to blow out

I hope you won't need
These wishes of mine
And you'll have many more
Of your own down the line
But this world is crazy
As I'm sure you can tell
So just in case
I'll wish these wishes right now

<u>You Are My Sunshine</u>

Your head is wrapped
In a helmet of gauze
Your eyes swollen shut
Your mouth makes no sound

You lie there limp
In your mother's embrace
A three month old bundle
With scars over your face

The problem was a tumor
Inside of your head
So they cut in deep
To dig it out

The result is the scene
Before my eyes
It is hard to observe
And not wonder why

Your mother gazes on
With love in her eyes

You are her only child
And nothing else matters

She requests that I play
"You Are My Sunshine"
Says she sings it to you
At home every night

I begin the song
In a melancholy key
After finishing one line
Tears stream down her cheeks

I am tempted to stop
But this somehow feels right
Your mom needs these tears
To cope with her plight

I leave your room
And wish all the best
It was doubtful that I
Would see you again

But ten months have passed
I run into mom
Still with tears in her eyes
And a look of fatigue

She shares the bad news
It didn't take long
Your body couldn't cope
And you have passed on

Although life is tough now
She wants me to know
She will always be grateful
For my song and my heart

It helped to bring peace
A moment of grace
She will cherish that time
For the rest of her life

As a moment when time
Had ceased to exist
Her little girl in her arms
A true moment of bliss

Joe the Buffalo

Joey was waiting in a grey, sterile room surrounded by adult cancer patients. Normally, a six year old patient would be surrounded by Disney cartoons and nurses in bright colored scrubs, but the pediatric floor was full and Joey needed his treatment today. He was easy to spot in the waiting room: a young, pale boy hunched in a ball next to his mother. His small figure made the room appear massive. A flat-brimmed baseball cap was trying to conceal the bald scalp beneath. He had superhero cartoon figures on his shirt, perhaps to give strength to his frail body. When I introduced myself, he nervously leaned into his mother and wrapped himself in her arm. Lately, whenever he met new people, they soon after wanted to poke him or cut him with scary implements of pain in the name of medicine.

To break the ice, I asked if he liked guitars. He remained silent, but his mother told me that they had just bought a second-hand guitar from a garage sale earlier that week. He wanted to learn how to play once he regained enough strength. "Do

23

you want me to teach you a few things?" I asked
him. He shyly nodded his head. I unstrapped my
guitar and gently laid it across his lap. Note by note,
I showed him how to play *Frère Jacques*. As he
played, a smile crept onto his face. Soon afterwards,
his smile turned into a grimace as he learned the
pain of playing guitar with sensitive, uncalloused
fingers. He handed me the guitar and asked me to
play.

After finishing a few songs, he asked me, "Do
you have any songs that you wrote? Do you want to
play one?" I had written a few songs in the past, but
they were quite rough and I did not think they were
very good. I had never played any of my own songs
for anyone except my wife, and that was difficult
enough. Looking at this poor boy's face, I could not
refuse. So I took a deep breath and swallowed my
embarrassment. I began to play what I thought was
my best song, but halfway through I forgot the
words and it ended with us all laughing. Joey
consoled me, telling me that he liked the song even
though I messed up. I was surprised at how quickly
we had switched roles.

As the flushing in my face began to resolve, I
had an idea. "Hey Joey, have you ever written a
song? Why don't we try writing one together?" He
loved the idea. I grabbed a pen from my pocket and
we began to write lyrics on the back of a song sheet

in my binder. We started the song by talking about his stuffed animal, Joe the Buffalo. Joey brought Joe with him to every scary procedure and Joe watched over him.

After we scratched this surface, Joey and his mom began to tell me about his experience with cancer. As they opened their souls to me, we worked together to create verses and rhymes and slowly built a song. He was diagnosed with leukemia one month before, and he was having a difficult time dealing with the dramatic changes this diagnosis entails. Although it had been a rough time so far, Joey had made some friends who also had cancer through a support group. This group had been a great help until last week, when one of Joey's new friends lost his battle. At the mere mention of his friend, tears began to roll down Joey's cheek. I waited until he was ready to go on.

He then told me that he was going to undergo a new procedure the next week. The idea of more new strangers and their medical devices was terrifying. Once Joey told me about the procedure, he began to cry harder and was inconsolable. He pulled the brim of his hat over his face and buried himself deeper into his mother's arms. It seemed apparent that we would get no further in our song, but I felt that I needed to wait for Joey. I needed to move at his pace. In a few minutes, Joey had calmed down enough to ask for a copy of the song. I made him a copy, but I saved one for myself as well.

This copy still sits in my music binder that I carry from room to room. It serves as a humbling reminder of a very meaningful experience. It is a reminder of my encounter with Joey and Joe the Buffalo.

Joe the Buffalo

[Chord progression – G, C, D, Am]

Joe is my buffalo
He's brown and hairy
Some people might think
He's kind of scary

He's my friend
He keeps me company
When I go to treatment
He's right there with me

Sometimes it's hard
Sometimes it's rough
Just keeping my chin up
Can be tough

Starting next week
They do a new procedure
They are doing lots of stuff
But I'm still not quite sure

By "Joey" and Bryan

Cleft Palate

The surgeon fixed your smile
But you haven't used it yet
A four year old girl
With a mouth full of pain
So I visit your bed to
Play you a song
And make all the noises
From Old MacDonald's farm
A sutured smile fights its way
Onto your face
A high pitched giggle
Escapes from within
For the moment the pain
Has gone from your lip
And you ask me to play
The song again

Relapse

In the first room I enter
Is a young boy I'd seen
For several months in the past
But not recently
"Look Mom, it's Bryan"
He yelled happily
"It's been such a long time
Since you last came to see me"
He showed me his Legos
And explained his game to me
As he played with his toys
His mother whispered quietly

"He relapsed in December,
His cancer came back
Now he's admitted for chemo
Four days at a time"
I solemnly nod
But keep my smile for him
Another painful reminder
Of why these sick kids come in

Of Cartoons and Humility

I enter her room, guitar in hand and ready to save the world. I introduce myself but the young eyes are fastened to the television screen. I ask this girl and her parents if they would like to hear any music. She is hesitant to respond so I wait. Her parents gently encourage her to respond; not pushing, just encouraging. She has been through too much today to be pushed. The young patient sneakily glances at me from the corner of her eye and I smile in return. Her eyes dart back to the television. One last time, her father asks her if she would rather watch television or listen to music. She replies, "I want to watch television *AND* listen to music." Finally, a compromise. We agree to turn down the volume while I play a song.

Next, we need to pick a song. Given the experience of the last few minutes, this promises to be another challenging task. I ask them if they would like to look through my binder of music, but they tell me to simply choose something that any eight year old girl would like. I flip towards the "Children's Music" section of my music binder and offer three different songs, but the young girl claims that she has never heard of any of them. I am not convinced, but I continue to smile and offer a fourth song. The girl yet again shakes her head. Her mother comes to my aid. "Oh, you do know that one. I heard you sing it at school." I ask the girl if she wants to hear this song and I receive a slight nod in return. This tiny affirmation is all that I needed. All I have to do now is play the song.

I start to strum the chord progression, trying to remember the tune. It must have been months since any patient has chosen this song. I quickly glance around the room before beginning. The mother is recording the session on her cell phone and the father is looking on with a smile. The young girl is looking at the television with a dispassionate stare. I wonder if she is secretly enjoying the music, or if I am simply interrupting her cartoon. I am inclined to believe the latter. As I begin to sing the song, my voice wavers around the correct key and I struggle to hit the notes. During the second verse of the song, my voice cracks, bringing back memories of pubertal embarrassment. I begin to realize that all of these mistakes are being recorded on the mother's cell phone. My confidence is sapped but I struggle through the remainder of the song with a smile on my face. With only one verse left, the IV alarm begins to beep. The infusion of chemotherapy is complete and a nurse enters the room. With the entry of the nurse, the child's face becomes completely blank. She has completely retreated into herself.

I have an excuse to end the song early and I take it. I thank the family and wish them the best of luck. There is no response from the young patient. She is not even looking at the television any more. She is merely holding her emesis basin and staring blankly at the floor. After leaving her room, I wander down the hallway and softly fingerpick some somber chords on my guitar. The different parts of my mind are attempting to understand the patient I just left.

My medical mind is curious about her diagnosis, her lab values, her prognosis. I begin to analyze her image as I have been trained to do with patients in clinic. She appeared quite ill. Her head was bald save for a narrow strip of short stubble near the crown. I wonder if these hairs were just growing in or on the verge of falling out. She does not appear too thin, so presumably she is early in her course of chemo. Her cheeks are not puffy, so she is not likely receiving corticosteroids. She is hugging an empty emesis basin. Is this a precaution or does she tolerate treatment poorly? What type of cancer does she have? Acute lymphocytic leukemia is the most common cancer in this age group. What is her prognosis? About 85% of patients with ALL will survive through the first five years after diagnosis. But that means 15% will not survive. Which group will she be in?

My emotional mind tries to understand the struggles this family must be experiencing. Does this young patient fully understand her diagnosis? Have her parents talked to her of the possibility of death? No, it must be too early for that. She still looks too healthy to think about death. Is she always in such a downcast mood or did they receive some bad news today? How are the parents coping? Do they feel helpless because they cannot protect their daughter? Do they have other children at home? What do the parents tell them? Do these siblings feel forgotten or left out? Will this trial pull the family together or will they become distant and fragmented?

My theological mind wonders if they have any religious beliefs. Do they believe in God? Do they go to church? Has their faith helped them to cope or has the cancer eaten away at their beliefs? Do they blame God? Do they question the existence of a God that allows innocent children to suffer from cancer? Is the problem of evil rearing its head in their lives?

As I stroll down the hallway, the many sides of my mind continue to postulate and create a story for this family. My speculation may be quite far from reality. Regardless, this story helps to untangle my thoughts. Why do I need this story? Does it help to bring me closer to this family and their suffering, or does it distance me from reality as though reading a sad novel? I do not know the answer, but I do know that it helps. That has to be enough for now. I pack up all of my questions and walk into the next room to meet another patient, hoping that my voice will not crack again.

Greek

We don't speak the same language
At least not in words
But through my guitar
We communicate well
You hear the message in my song
Regardless of my foreign tongue
Your smile sends a message in return
Without your mouth uttering a word

Music is a Rosetta Stone
Accessible to all, a gift of hope
Music can break boundaries
And commune our hearts and souls
Music has great power
That language never will

Language

Playing for a family
From far overseas
They smile and nod
In rhythm with me
As I finish my stint
And prepare to leave
They think quite hard
And say to me
The only English phrase
They happen to know
"Thank you very much"
    And it was enough

Amazing Grace

Slider stole my patients. The Cleveland Indians mascot was visiting patients at the Children's Hospital today, and my guitar was no competition for his bright costume and free toys. I was relegated to seeing only one patient, a twenty year old young woman accompanied by her mother. As I entered her room, she was sitting in a recliner with a blanket draped over her legs. Her body was relaxed except for her right arm where she was receiving an infusion of chemotherapy. She held this arm rigidly extended, trying to keep it perfectly straight. The alarm on her IV had been intermittently beeping for the last hour. Each time, the same warning appeared on the screen: *Occlusion*. This meant that the IV catheter inside of her vein was becoming obstructed. If the tube became completely blocked, then the nurse would have to start a new IV line, meaning more needle pokes. Despite the problems with her IV, her face beamed with warmth and contentment. I introduced myself and asked if they wanted to hear any music.

"Oh sure, that'd be great," she responded with a smile. She slowly flipped through my stack of music. "Oh my gosh, mom, look at this! He *has* to play this one. I used to sing this all the time when I was little." I began to play and they all sang with me. During the last chorus, her IV pole began to harshly beep. The nurse came in again to flush the IV with saline, trying to coax it into patency. It seemed to cooperate, so the nurse restarted the infusion and left us to our music. Over the next forty minutes we played through a slew of songs, each one interrupted by intermittent occlusions and alarms.

After the seventh alarm sounded, the flustered nurse decided to start a new IV line in her other arm. She apologetically shared the plan with the patient. I expected her to flinch or feel upset at the prospect of another needle stick, but she freely offered her other arm without paying any attention to the invasive needle searching for a vein. "I had a really bad infection a while back... the chemo really trashes my immune system. Anyways, they stuck me over twenty times in one day while I was in the hospital. So this stuff doesn't really bother me anymore." I was impressed by her calm. I still cringed at the mere thought of a flu shot. After a few pokes, the nurse successfully landed in a vein and restarted the infusion. Once the nurse had finished, the patient began to share her story with me.

"I was first diagnosed with cancer when I was pretty young. Back then, the doctors all kept telling me that I wouldn't live through my teens... but here I am." She had survived, but it was not an easy journey. Her story over the past decade was a sine wave of relapses and remissions. She was at a peak just a few weeks ago, but now she was quickly sliding into the trough. Each relapse meant a new round of chemotherapy, which inevitably led to a bald head, a weak body and horrendous mouth sores.

"That must have been a lot to deal with. How did you manage?" I asked.

"It was tough at times, really tough. But my family and my friends always reminded me that I needed to keep on living my life. We figured that if I was still alive, I might as well make the most of my time." And she had made the most of it. She recounted numerous stories of road trips to concerts, skydiving, college adventures, getting engaged. She was wringing every bit of joy from her life. "You know, I don't know how much more time I have left, but nobody really does. Any of us could get hit by a bus, and that would be the end of it. At least I got a heads up. My diagnosis wasn't a death sentence. It was a reminder that I need to live my life while I still have it."

I could not think of a response. I simply strummed my guitar and thought about my own life. How often did I focus on the difficulties and challenges in my life rather than the blessings? How much time did I spend planning for the future while ignoring the here and now? Just before coming to the hospital that day, I was worried about things like board exams, grants, assessments, research projects, publications, a stain on my shirt. How do these things compare to the genuine problems of this patient? As she said, I could be run over by a bus and none of these trivialities would matter. There is no better equalizer than an errant bus. Life is a borrowed gift. We are all going to die someday, whether we acknowledge that fact or not. And if I disappeared tomorrow, the world would continue to spin just as it has for billions of years. I am merely a speck among specks on a pebble that is hurtling through space. The world is much larger than any individual.

After recovering from my brief reverie, I sincerely thanked the patient for sharing her story. "I think you have really helped to open my eyes to a few things." I allowed these words to float around the room before I spoke again. "How about one more song?" I asked. They flipped through my stack of music and chose a song from the very bottom. They requested *Amazing Grace*, and we sang together with eyes closed. I had to hold back tears as we moved through the verses of this powerful song. I thought it very suiting that this young woman chose *Amazing Grace*; that was the best way I could describe her approach to setbacks in life.

Like clockwork, the IV alarm erupted in a shrill song as we finished the last verse. The frustrated nurse rushed in to stop the howling. While she worked on the mischievous pump, I thanked the family once again and left the room. After packing up my guitar, I slowly walked down the stairs to the main lobby of the hospital. With each step, I could feel the world of deadlines and expectations slowly descending upon my shoulders. I stopped in the stairwell and closed my eyes. I imagined the world continuing to spin. I imagined a speck among specks on a pebble that was hurtling through space. I imagined an errant bus. Suddenly the weight on my shoulders seemed less.

Git-tar Boy

Six months have passed
Since we first met
A young girl trapped
In her hospital bed
And a med student volunteer
With guitar in hand
We sang a few songs
Before I moved along

But now she's returned
The same problem with her brain
Despite the new meds
Her seizures won't quit
So they pulled her from school
And brought her back North
From her Appalachian home
To this city on the lake
She's here "for observation"
Meaning no plan yet
But she can't leave the hospital
Until she seizes for them

I doubt she'll remember
It's been so long
Since I came to her room
And played her a song
But as I walk to her door
Her nurse stops me to say
"She was asking for you,
The very first thing"
In a sweet twangy voice
She had asked with a smile
"Where is that git-tar boy
That played for me before?"
She remembered me still
Despite distance and time
And she wanted some music
To help ease her mind

It's hard to believe that
A song can do much
To offset the plight that
These kids have to bear
But maybe it's more
To such families in need
Maybe my presence
Lets them know that I care
Maybe my heart can pour
Out through my songs

And at least for a moment
Help them to stay strong
I don't know the answers
But they'll have to wait
There's still a girl in that room
Who wants her git-tar boy to play

Surprise Ending

Entering a room to offer a song
I meet a teenage boy,
He is blind but refuses
His mother's help as
He methodically flips through
The pages of music,
Scrutinizing each sheet
With his blank eyes,
"How about this one?" he asks
Seemingly at random,
I read the title and artist
He assents with a nod
So I pick the strings and
Sing along,
When the notes hit his ears
He lays back his head
With a rapt smile attached
And seems to rest,
At the end he returns
To the stack of songs
Selecting several more
Before the visit was done,

During our last tune
As I play away
His body suddenly stiffens
With neck unnaturally arched
A groan escapes his lips
Starting low but
Increasing in pitch,
His mother quickly recognizes
This recurrent scene,
Jumps to hit the
Magic red button
The seizure alarm that signals
An influx of medical staff,
Not sure what to say
Or what to do
I slowly back out
Of the room

"Go Bess Ooo"

Strumming through the hall
I meet a little girl and her mom
I stop and offer
To play them a song
I pick a classical tune
And watch their smiles grow
They relax as the music
Helps to lighten their load
Once I finish the song
The mother gratefully says
"Thank you and God bless you"
And she shakes my hand
Then her two year old girl
With eyes that swallow my heart
Smiles widely and says
"Go Bess Ooo" just like her mom

Cardboard Guitar

No one knew Mason had epilepsy until a few weeks ago when he suddenly developed a seizure. The next day, his parents drove him hundreds of miles to this Children's Hospital where he has been held captive ever since. As nurses and doctors continuously cycled through his hospital room, his parents desperately tried to absorb all the information and orders that flew through the air. While his family learned to cope with his new disease, Mason merely toiled the days away in his hospital bed.

In the midst of this haze, I entered his room and asked if they wanted to hear any music. Mason had just recovered from yet another seizure. His eyes had the characteristic post-ictal, puffy glaze and he looked exhausted, but his parents assured me that he wanted me to play. He was not fully lucid but coherent enough to choose a few songs. As we played and sang together, Mason haphazardly shook some egg-shakers and his father drummed on an empty ice bucket. After a few songs, Mason had run out of energy, so I packed up my music and left.

His condition worsened over the next week, so he was moved to the pediatric intensive care unit (PICU). The seizures had become more stubborn and would not respond to medications. Mason was having between ten and twenty seizures each day, and sometimes the seizures would not stop. This number of seizures put Mason at significant risk for sudden death. His brain and his body could have given out at any point, leaving his family with one less little boy. With extra medical staff, monitoring systems and crash carts in each room, the PICU was equipped to handle his situation.

When I visited Mason in the PICU, wires and tubes poured out from all the crevices of his body. Beeping machines with numbers and graphs crowded the tiny room. The sight was intimidating to a young medical student. I avoided touching anything for fear of setting off an explosion of alarms and receiving angry scowls from the nurses. I carefully handed the stack of music to Mason while maneuvering around the machinery. After Mason had chosen his favorite songs, I began to sing in very hushed tones, hoping not to disturb the other sick children on the floor. My voice was hardly loud enough to cut through the droning symphony of life preserving equipment in the room, but Mason and his mother were still thankful for the brief diversion.

49

Over the next week, the physicians barraged Mason's body with every available therapy short of brain surgery. Slowly, the seizures began to subside. Once Mason was stable enough, he was moved back to his original room on the pediatrics floor. Within minutes of his return, he went to work decorating every square inch with handmade crafts. The walls were adorned with crayon-drawn pictures of dinosaurs and airplanes, and every doorknob and handle was decorated with a lopsided foam door hanger. As I entered the room, Mason was buried under a mountain of construction paper fallout and his hands were stained by wayward marker swipes. The tips of his fingers were caked with half-dried glue and lint from every corner of the room. He looked up and smiled at me as I walked through the door, then quickly returned to his work.

"Do you want to hear Bryan play some music?" asked Mason's mother. He nodded without raising his eyes from his newest creation-in-progress. I handed Mason's mother my stack of music, and we followed the same routine we had established over the previous month. After playing through a few songs, Mason's mother stopped me.

"Oh, Mason, we almost forgot. Don't you want to show Bryan your surprise?"

"Yeah! Yeah! Yeah!" Mason's eyes widened in excitement as he responded. His mother quickly rummaged through a large pile of toys and clothes in the corner of the room. After a few seconds of searching, she pulled out what looked like a cardboard box. It was the leftover packaging from one of the many toys Mason had accumulated in the hospital. There were five rubber bands stretched around the length of the box, each one evenly spaced from the others. Every rubber band was a different color: red, green, yellow, blue, orange. The sides of the box had been painted brown and the inside of the box was white. It was no longer a box; it was now Mason's guitar.

He beamed with pride as his mother handed him the instrument. Over the next few minutes, he described in detail the process of making a guitar: finding a box, painting it, letting it dry, drawing designs, finding rubber bands. He explained that he only used five strings because there were only five different colors of rubber bands. After complimenting the quality of his instrument, I suggested that we play a song together. As I began to strum, I noticed that my guitar string was flat so I began to adjust the tuning key. Out of the corner of my eye, I noticed that Mason was also tuning his guitar. He stretched and tightened the strings as he plucked each rubber band with his other hand.

After a few attempts, his guitar was finally "in tune", but then he noticed something else that was different about our guitars. His guitar was missing a sound hole. He asked his mother for a pair of scissors to fix the discrepancy. She cautiously handed him a pair of safety scissors and helped him to cut a sound hole in the back of the box.

The box twisted and bent in every direction as he tried to cut through the thick cardboard. I was worried that his guitar would not survive to play another song. After a few tenuous moments, the back of the box had a jagged and uneven opening. Once he finished cutting the hole, we played one last song together: me on steel strings, Mason on rubber bands. His fingers clumsily plucked and strummed a pattern and a cacophony of noise sprung from the box. His face beamed with the intent look of a master musician; my face was fixed with an uncontrollable smile. Regardless of the noise others might have heard, Mason and I knew that we were creating beautiful music.

After finishing the song, Mason took a deep breath and finally smiled. We took a bow and his mother loudly applauded our performance. After receiving this praise, his eyes began to droop and he laid his head back in exhaustion. He had put his heart and soul into the song, and now the master musician needed rest. His mother gently ran her hand through Mason's hair and gave him a kiss on his forehead. I quietly said goodbye and backed out of the room.

A Loaded Word

Developmental delays
And defects abounded
Glazed, sunken eyes
Stared blandly ahead
Scalp sparsely peppered
With unsightly tufts
Lips pocked with blisters
Screamed out in pain
His fingers were covered
With calloused scales
An eight year old boy
With eighty year old hands

Hunched with indifference
Until hearing my song
He gasped with intrigue
And shot from his chair
Holding his face
Inches from my guitar
He could smell the music
As I continued to strum

His excitement grew and
He danced in place
A few chords later
He wanted to try
His small grizzled hand
Gently plucked at each string
While my fingers changed chords
And built him a song
As the sounds rang out
His smile grew wider
The pace grew quicker and
The plucking stronger
His mother feared
He would hurt the guitar
I told her no worries
And let him play on

While he picked and he strummed
His mom filled me in
They were from a small town
Just an hour due South
He was in special school
Just started third grade
Was doing so well
Until cancer arrived
He loved to hear music
Especially guitar

Back home his visitor
Would bring one along
And she'd let him strum
Just like he did now
It gave him great joy
To create his own song
I ask her who plays
This music back home
And in her reply she
Lets the word out
With such gravity and meaning
That it fell with a thud
"His hospice nurse plays
When she comes to our house"

Hospice means no cure,
Terminal, death
My poor little friend
Has no options left
That loaded word
Hits my heart like a brick
But I keep a stone face
With a smile carved in
He is going to die,
There is no recourse
With no magic bullet,
No miracle in sight

Is music the last hope
That remains for this boy?
A prescription to enrich
His shortened life?
I can't cure his ills,
But I offer some joy
In the form of a song
And a smiling face
I'm not that important,
But I do play my part
I can't give him a cure
But I can share my heart

Johnny

Johnny is gone
He passed last week
It took us all by surprise
It took me by surprise

I saw him every week
For several months
He always came to clinic with
A backwards hat covering
His smooth, sensitive scalp
Never wanting any music
But always wanting to talk
We came to be friends
Little by little
Week by week

He was taking courses at
A local college
Trying to live his life
Trying to ignore the elephant
Trampling his house
Now he's suddenly gone

Like he passed through a rift
In the earth
Never to walk the halls again
Never to joke with the nurses
At the front desk
Never to give a warm hello
That brightens days
No, he is gone
And I feel sad

Sad for his family
 And his friends
Sad that we'll never
 Talk again
Sad because I didn't
 Get to know him more
Sad because cancer
 Won this war
Sad because Johnny
 Was only twenty three
Scared because that's nearly
 The same age as me

Expectations

Brie never wanted any music. Every week I offered, and every week she hid behind her father and whispered a gentle rejection. This pattern repeated for nearly two months. Each interaction had the same conclusion: she would decline and I would put on a smile to cover my disappointment as I walked from her examination room. Regardless, I would always return the following week with another offer for a song. After a few weeks, I was merely asking out of principle. I knew she would say no, but my conscience felt better for asking.

I was expecting much the same today when I walked towards her room. She was sitting in a tiny chair at a low table working on a coloring book. Her face was intently focused as she struggled to keep her crayon tip within the lines. She was transforming a bland butterfly into an explosion of bright colors. Following my usual pattern, I asked if she wanted to play any music. With my expectations set, I braced myself for her response.

"No," she replied, "but do you want to color with me?" This was the first time I had heard her voice at a volume above a whisper. The shy girl from previous weeks was gone. Like her butterfly, she was displaying her newly found colors. I did not know what triggered the change, but I gladly sat down and she handed me a crayon. We flipped to a picture of a bunny and began to plan our coloring strategy.

"You color the ears pink, and I'll color the nose blue," she commanded. Following her orders, I carefully filled the ears with color. As I was working, she looked at my progress and said, "You're really good at staying in the lines." This was high praise indeed. After a few minutes of coloring and following further orders, we had finished the rabbit. It looked like the product of a tie-dye explosion. She tore the masterpiece from the coloring book and stuffed it into her pink backpack. Just as we finished the piece, her IV pump began to beep, signaling that her chemotherapy infusion was complete. The nurse walked in to disconnect her IV and send her home.

While the nurse worked, I stepped out of the room and walked down the hall in search of more patients. The other examination rooms were all closed or empty, so I casually paced the hallway and played a tune to myself. A few minutes later, my pacing carried me by the little artist's room yet again. She was standing in the doorway with her arms crossed as the nurse spoke with her father. "Hey little lady," I said with a smile. "How's it going?" She took a few steps towards me and stopped short with uncertainty in her face. After a slight hesitation, she embarrassedly asked, "Well, why don't you just give me a hug, already?" I bent down and she wrapped her little arms over my guitar and around my neck. A physician was walking down the hall and commented with a grin, "Well, isn't that just the nicest gift?" She was absolutely right.

It was hard to believe she was the same little girl who had avoided me for the last seven weeks. I never imagined that I would connect with her by setting aside my guitar and picking up a crayon. But life often takes these sorts of turns. Some of the most blessed moments are those that deviate from my preconceived plans and notions. My expectations must be disappointed at times in order to remind me that I cannot control my life, I can only live it. Although some of these experiences will be good and others bad, life would be much less meaningful without these graceful inconveniences.

Three Little Birds

I enter the room and
Offer a song
To a Jamaican family
A long way from home
This young patient's family
Is all at hand
Brother sister mom dad
Cousin uncle and aunt
It takes a village to raise a child
The proof is in this room

They ask if I can play
A Bob Marley song
But I haven't learned any
On the guitar
They hide their disappointment
But it hangs in the air
While the room steeps in silence
I sit down in a chair,
Flip the guitar over,
And drum a Marley tune

About three little birds that know
It will be alright soon
I search my mind for the words
And begin to sing
But after only two lines
The room was singing with me
They emptied their hearts
While holding back the tears
And used this song
To vanquish their fears

Dancing

Nothing warms my heart
Like a chubby baby girl
With cheeks billowing
Around her pacifier
Dancing and rocking
Side to side
Shaking her whole body
In rhythm with my song
Then pulling out her pacifier
Just so long
To show her gummy smile
Hidden beneath

The Empty Hallway

I walk through the hallway
With guitar in arms
Hoping for a stranger
In need of a song
My guitar strings are yearning
To sing out loud
And my fingers are restless
As I search for a crowd
I look in each room
And knock on the doors
But the patients have vanished
From this entire floor

I ask the charge nurse
Where the patients have gone
She slowly turns to the board,
Puts her reading glasses on
"Bed 1 is getting a CT scan
Bed 2 an X-ray of his chest
Bed 3's been empty all week long
Bed 4 in surgery, Bed 5 just left

My excitement is sapped
When she finishes this list
Of the kids on the floor
That I just missed
My shoulders sag
But I try not to pout
As I pass the empty hallway
On my way out
I slowly pack my guitar
Back into its case
My diversion has disappeared,
Reality stares me in the face

Magic Guitar

"I wouldn't go in there if I were you." The nurses were always looking out for me. "The patient is barely a year old, and he is blind and developmentally delayed. Plus, he only understands Chinese. But if you want to try, feel free." I took a moment to consider this warning, but ultimately decided to take the risk. The worst case scenario was that the mother would send me away.

I softly tapped on the door and entered the dark hospital room. The mother was seated in a chair holding a book, but her eyes were focused on her son. The little boy was rolling around on his back in bed, discovering the invisible world around him with his busy fingertips. His bed was surrounded by a cage of thick steel bars that protected him from falling, but also made him look like a prisoner of the hospital. As my eyes adjusted to the darkness of the room, I introduced myself to the mother.

"Hi, my name is Bryan. I am a medical student, but I play guitar at the hospital every week. Would you two like to hear any music?" The

68

mother gave me a suspicious look and asked in broken English, "What music you play?"

"Well, I can play a lot of different kinds of music," I responded with a smile. "I have a stack of songs here, but I can also play something instrumental, without words, if you would prefer."

She considered my proposal for a few seconds before cautiously consenting. "I think you should play no words, just guitar." With her approval, I began to fingerpick a classical guitar song. Once I plucked the first few notes, the little boy sat up in bed and "looked" through his blind eyes directly into mine. I could have sworn that he was staring at me, taking in the surprised look on my face. His busy fingers stood still and a smile grew on his lips as he sat transfixed by the music. The mother's coldness melted when she saw how her son enjoyed the music. After I finished the first song, the mother urged me to play another. Once I plucked through the next song, the mother said "I never hear music like that before. You change my mind." My face showed her that I did not comprehend her meaning. She continued, "I never hear guitar that way before. I always thought guitar music loud and ugly, and I not like it. But you change my mind. Your music is very beautiful." She went on, "I have older son, and my husband want him play guitar. I say no because I thought guitar bad. I only want him learn piano or violin. But now I hear you play, I think I let him learn guitar… only if he play like you." After hearing this compliment, I felt tinges of embarrassment and was unsure how to respond. I had never been good at accepting compliments. I simply smiled, said thank you, and began to play another song. Once I finished, I thanked the mother and son and wished them the best of luck. The mother thanked me again as I backed out of the room.

When I emerged into the hallway, I caught the eyes of the protective nurse. "How did it go in there?" she asked.

"Just fine," I replied with a smile and a gentle nod of my head. "They really enjoyed the music." As I recounted my story, the look on her face showed that she was happily surprised.

"Well, I'll be darned… you must have a magic guitar," she replied. "She hasn't smiled since the day they came to the hospital." She smiled and shook her head. "Since that worked out so well, would you mind seeing the patient in bed 7? She is having a really rough day, but maybe some music would help her, too." I gladly agreed and walked toward the patient's room, strumming the magic guitar.

Gracefully

Your arm is turning blue
And you are losing motor control
The tumor is growing into the nerves
And blocking the veins

The cancer has taken so much from you
You cannot sing with the tumor in your lungs
You cannot play guitar with the tumor in your arm
You cannot swallow with the tumor in your throat
You cannot sleep with the tumor in your neck

Never before have you asked for help
But yesterday you couldn't shave
Your arm just hung there
Like rotting fruit ready to fall from the tree

This disease has ruined so many things
But you handle it so well
You calmly predict 6 to 8 weeks left
Willing to face the facts
You say your faith will carry you through

And give you strength
It seems it already has

To die gracefully is a task one
Cannot practice
There is only one try
Through your calm suffering
You have become the archetype

You sit under the stars at night
Not embarrassed by your tears
You follow a shooting star
And drift off to sleep

A Reason to Smile

How many miles from
Denmark to here?
How many hours? How many layovers?
How many cab rides? How many worries?
How much did it cost to travel?
Distance was the cost, distance geographic
And distance of the heart.

His parents could not leave their work,
But Uncle's job could wait.
Along he came these four thousand miles
With his teenage nephew,
Over North Sea, Celtic Sea, Atlantic Ocean
Resting finally at the Great Lakes,
From salt water to fresh,
From the Scandinavian fingers to
This storied institution,
This healthcare Mecca of the West,
A Mecca for epileptics.

He was carted through endless hallways,
And placed in a room of plastic and steel.

The nurse glued leads and wires
To every exposed scrap of skin.
Each wire connected to a different monitor,
Each monitor told a different story:
One, a tale of his heart rhythm,
Another, his temperamental brain,
Another, a poem of his blood pressure
Set to the music of his pulse.
All the while, a video camera surveyed,
Big brother watching for a seizure.
He was given a private room;
Private – the ultimate misnomer,
His breezy gown did not speak of privacy,
Nor the endless stream of well-meaning staff
That poked and prodded at all hours.
Even the hidden stories of his internal organs
Were displayed on monitors for all to see.

He had been in bed for three days when
I first came to visit, guitar in hand.
We played several songs,
The room full of smiles and laughs.
We spoke of Denmark and Medicine,
Philosophy and Life;
Uncle taught me the proper pronunciation
Of Kierkegaard
They were in high spirits when I left
As was I.

Two weeks passed until I saw him next.
The seizures had not ceased, but the docs
Had found their source, a spot in his brain
That started those disastrous waves.
So they shaved his head, cut his skin,
Opened the skull, and dug out brain,
That aberrant focus of electrical noise.

He was two days post-op
When I returned to the floor.
A nurse stopped me with warning
As I walked toward his door:
Since undergoing surgery
His behavior had changed,
He refused to eat or take his meds,
And his temper easily flared.
Earlier, he threw a cup of ice cream
At his flustered nurse,
Then he threw harsh words
To chase her from sight.
I walked into his room, expecting the worst.

A turban of bandages decorated his head
Completely hiding the C-shaped incision,
His eyes were swollen, tired, and red,
His lips drooped without motor control.
I said hello and re-introduced myself,

Not sure if his memory was intact.
He said he remembered and
He was glad I came back.
He asked for some songs, I gladly began.
As my guitar sang out in notes and chords
He rested his head and closed his eyes,
His shoulders relaxed
As he relished the sound.
Thirty minutes passed with several songs,
Then it was time to visit other rooms.
As I said goodbye and walked toward the door
He stopped me with a soft word,
He had a parting message for me,
A gift he hoped to give.
With labored words that fought his accent
And his paralyzed lips, he said
"Your music is one
Of the only things
That makes me want to smile.
I only wish
My lips could move
To show you that it's true"

This Machine Kills Pain

Walking along
      Plucking a song
This Land is Your Land
      Jumps out from my hand
Singing the words of old Woody
      A thought comes to me
His guitar killed fascists
      With bold letters hardly missed
Although not quite the same
      Maybe my guitar kills pain

To My Guitar

Badly warped face
Bridge pulling off
Battle earned scars
From hospital walls
Strings tough to hold down
Impossible to bend
But this cheap guitar
Taught me to play
And brought so much joy
To sick kids in bed
Giving them smiles
Displacing their dread
It followed me over the country
From East Coast to West
Resting on my shoulder
In its ragged patched case
It's survived many adventures
Collecting scratches but intact
And I'll keep playing this guitar
    Until the bridge finally cracks

I Can't Write No Song

A plastic heart was hanging from his gauze-wrapped chest, rhythmically propelling blood through his body. The child life specialist had told me his story before I came to visit: this eight year old boy had a disease that destroyed his heart, and he had been waiting eight months for a transplant. Unfortunately, his heart was not strong enough to support him while he waited. His best option was the external device that sat in his lap, taking over the duties of his dying heart. This plastic pump was connected to a refrigerator-sized box next to his bed that monitored blood flow, pressure and oxygenation. The tubing that connected him to the box was a leash that allowed him to reach the bathroom, but not any further. Once a week, he and his heart would take a walk while a team of nurses pushed his box through the hospital. Other than these vacations, he had been trapped in his room for eight months without seeing the outside world or smelling fresh air.

With a guitar on my back, I knocked on the door and this young boy signaled for me to come in.

"Hi Jake, I'm Bryan. I play music at the hospital every week. Your child life specialist told me that you might be interested in learning to play guitar. What do you think? Do you want to give it a try?" I chose not to tell him I was a medical student, hoping our relationship would help to distract him from all his medical issues. He excitedly nodded his head in response to my offer and we started the lessons.

Initially, we began by naming the parts of the guitar and numbering the frets and strings, but his attention quickly dissipated and he wanted to play a song. So I took off my guitar and Jake laid it across his lap, resting it on top of the blood-filled tubes poking from his chest. Within a few seconds of this maneuvering, a shrieking alarm sounded, telling us that Jake was cutting off the blood flow from his second heart. I felt panic rising up inside me, ready to shout for a nurse from the hallway, but Jake merely said, "Don't worry, my tubes are just kinked." He indifferently grabbed and untwisted his heart tubes, not concerned that he was holding his life source in his hands. Perhaps humans can adapt to any situation with enough time.

Once he finished adjusting the tubes, I began to teach him a simple song. His hands were not strong enough to press the strings down by himself, so I placed my fingers next to his and we played through part of the song. His fingers soon began to ache and he could not press the strings anymore, so I held the chords with my left hand as he strummed the guitar. We made our way through another part of the song before he stopped again.

"Do you have any picks?" he asked. I did not, so we looked around the room for a substitute. After a short search, he found a wooden tongue depressor, broke a small piece off and began to strum the guitar again. At the end of our song, he asked me to play one by myself. I began to hit the strings with my fingers, but he stopped me again and said, "You need a pick too." He broke off another piece of the tongue depressor and gave me a custom-made pick to use for the rest of the day.

His attention span seemed to last about the length of one song before his interest shifted to something new. When I finished playing the song, he asked me if I wanted to write a song with him.

"I'd love to write a song together. What do you want to write about?" I asked.

"I'm not sure... I don't even know if I can write a song..." he responded.

"Well that sounds like a great line for our song! *I can't write no song, The words won't get on that page.*" I played a bluesy riff as we added more lyrics, and pretty soon we had created the first verse of the song. After laying down this portion of the song, it was time for me to visit other patients. I

81

promised to visit him the following week to work on his guitar lessons and our song. He gave me a high-five as I left his room.

The next week, Jake had his own guitar when I came to visit, a gift from the hospital. It was a blue beginner guitar constructed of flimsy wood and cheap plastic tuners. When he began to strum, I noticed that the guitar was horribly out of tune. I used this as an opportunity to teach him how to tune his instrument. We switched guitars and he plucked the individual strings while I adjusted the tuning knobs. Once the guitar was in tune, I tried to hand him back his guitar, but he asked if he could use mine for a while. I smiled and gladly strummed on his little blue guitar. Throughout my visit, we wrote another verse for our song and played through a few others. In the middle of one song, he was having difficulty holding down the strings and he quit out of frustration. Trying to encourage him, I said, "It takes time to learn guitar, buddy. But you're getting a big head start by starting so young. I didn't pick up a guitar until I was twenty years old. That means that you have a twelve year head start on me. Just imagine how good you will be when you are my age!" He smiled at my reasoning.

Over the next few months, I continued to see Jake every week in his hospital room. With each visit, his guitar skills improved and we eventually made it through entire songs without needing to stop. We also added more lyrics to our song each week until we felt that it was finished. Once the song was complete, I told Jake about my plan.

"I've got a gig in a few weeks, and I would love to play our song for the crowd. I could even record the performance and send you a CD with the song. What do you think? Are you okay with that?" I asked.

"That sounds cool, but just make sure you tell them that we *both* wrote the song." I gladly agreed to his terms.

Things continued much the same way until just before Christmas. During my last week in town before leaving for the holiday, my schedule had become very erratic. I had to cancel and reschedule my usual session with Jake twice during the week because of conflicting meetings that popped up. Finally, I scheduled a visit with Jake for later in the week, the last day that I was in town before leaving for vacation. Then at the last minute, another meeting forced its way into my schedule during the time when I was supposed to see Jake. Initially I decided to skip his visit for the week. I was busy and stressed, and even if I skipped lunch, I would have only had about fifteen minutes to spend with him. It seemed futile to spend more time walking to his room than I would in his room. I made up my mind to skip the session until after the holiday, but something did not feel right. My decision bothered me throughout the day. At the last minute, I decided to visit him anyway. Fifteen minutes were better than no minutes. I grabbed my guitar case and rushed to his room.

When I arrived, a few nurses were standing around his bed with tears in their eyes. My heart seemed to stop, and I imagined that something terrible had happened. I walked slowly towards his bed, prepared to hear bad news. With wet eyes, Jake said, "Guess what I'm going to get for Christmas. Something I've been waiting ten months for. They found me a heart… a perfect match." After hearing the news, I began to breathe normally again, but his words were not filled with excitement as I had expected. Instead, they sounded nervous and fearful. Over the last eleven months, he had grown accustomed to his lifestyle in the hospital, and leaving must have been a scary proposition. Also, he was about to head into a very serious operation within the next few hours where someone else's heart would be sewn into his body. These circumstances would be difficult for anyone to bear, much less an eight year-old boy. I was not sure exactly what to say or how to feel, so I merely ruffled his hair and congratulated him.

"That's great news! How do you feel about it?" I asked.

"I don't know... Pretty scared, I guess," he responded, his eyes gazing at the floor. I sat there with him on the bed and waited for him to talk again. "Well, do you want to play some music?" he finally asked. After this signal, we tuned guitars and began to play the song we had written. As we played, our audience grew. Nurses, art therapists and child life specialists began to pour into the room to hear our concert. At the end of the song, applause and whistles filled the air and we took a bow together.

After twenty minutes had passed, I had to pry myself away from the room to get to my meeting on time. Jake gave me a big hug and I congratulated him again. I walked out of the room unsure how to feel. Everyone knew that his situation had to change eventually, but the news was still surprising when it came. As I left his room that day, I kept thinking about Jake's future. He was so fortunate to have found a suitable heart, but how long would his transplant last? How would he cope with taking immunosuppressive medications for the rest of his life? How would his family bear the expense of medications? In the future, would this affect his ability to get health insurance? To get a job? Would his new heart get in the way of making friends and developing relationships? There were many questions, but only time held the answers.

Over the next few days, I continued to worry about Jake and his operation. Eventually, Jake's child life specialist informed me that Jake's surgery was a success, and that he was recovering quite well. I returned the next week to find that he had been moved to a different floor of the hospital. When I entered his new room, he was lying in bed, his chest covered by a hospital gown without any tubes poking out of it. His mother was sitting beside his bed and I introduced myself to her. It was the first time we had met, but she had heard much about our guitar lessons from Jake and the hospital staff. She thanked me for spending so much time with Jake, telling me how much it had helped him through the last few months. After accepting her thanks, I turned to Jake.

"How are you feeling? You look like a free man!" I said. Although he was smiling, he was not his normal outgoing self. He merely shrugged and said, "I'm alright. I guess it's cool to be able to walk anywhere I want to now." It was apparent that Jake was still adjusting to his newfound freedom, not sure whether to be happy or sad. To break the tension, Jake's mother asked if he wanted to show me his new Christmas present. His mood suddenly changed and he excitedly said, "Okay, but you have to turn around and close your eyes!" I followed his orders and waited. When I opened my eyes, Jake was holding a new electric guitar in his hands.

"He's really taken to playing guitar, so we are going to continue his lessons back home," his mother told me. "It's been really great for him, and I hope he keeps at it." Jake then proudly proceeded to show me all of the features on his new guitar, from one end to the other. Once he had shown me every square inch of the instrument, we tuned up and played our song together one last time. Unlike before, there was no influx of audience members from the hallway and no raucous applause at the end. We were playing only for ourselves, closing this chapter of his life as he started on the next one. Once the song ended, we said our farewells and each went our separate ways: him towards recovery and me towards another patient's room.

I Can't Write No Song

I've been thinking 'bout playing guitar
But I just can't do it
Seems like every time I try it
My fingers just want to quit
This old guitar has really got me down

Well I'm pushing down those strings
But they just make me yell
And I can't even tune it
I'm so mad I can't even tell
Why'd I ever spend money, on this stupid old guitar

And I can't write no song
The words won't get on that page
And I can't hold no tune
It really gives me pain
Why'd I ever get up here, on this big scary stage

You don't even want to hear me
You might as well just run out
Cause if I start singin'
That glass will shatter and fall
I can't believe you all came here, just to hear me yell

By "Jake" and Bryan

Afterword

There are times in life when the stars seem to inexplicably align, and serendipity enriches our lives. Today was such a day. This was my last session playing guitar at the Children's Hospital, a day I entered with a heavy heart prepared for many farewells. Regardless, I strapped on my guitar like usual and began to wander in search of an audience. As I walked through the familiar outpatient hallway, I happened to see the mother of Laney, the young girl from the first story in this collection. She immediately gave me a warm hug that only mothers know how to give, heart to heart. Then she told me, "Now you always remember, you're my baby too up here in Cleveland. You're family." She asked me about my school, my wife, my life. I updated her as we walked towards Laney's exam room.

After entering the room, I quietly stood in the doorway and waited, not saying anything until Laney turned around and saw me. When she recognized me, her surprised eyes opened wide and a smile burst across her face. She was three years older than when I had first met her, paralyzed and mute in her post-op bed. This young girl had turned into a young woman before my eyes. She was still using a walker, but the therapists were helping her to transition to a cane. Her language skills were improving, and her vision was getting better by the day. She and her mother were finally reaching their new normal.

"Alright baby, now why don't you walk over to Bryan and give him a hug?" said Laney's mother. With this encouragement, she let go of her walker and took several small, unassisted steps towards me. She walked across the width of the room with only the strength of her legs and her heart, slowly wobbling into my arms and giving me an eye-watering hug. Her mother said, "You just don't understand how much you helped her through those first few months. You've done so much for her, and that's why we love you." There have been few moments in my life when I was so completely speechless, but words simply could not suffice to express three years of emotions. Instead, I merely smiled and soaked in the love from my adopted family.

Over the next several minutes, Laney and her mother told me about her future plans. Laney had just graduated eighth grade, and she was excited for the transition to high school. She told me that she wanted to be a professional chef when she finished all of her schooling. After this, she explained that she wanted to have 15 kids, and she wanted to have 15 puppies too, one for each child. But her mom mentioned how expensive children are, and how little chefs earn as a salary, so she changed her mind to having only two kids.

As I listened to her dreams pour out into the air, I remembered my first image of her, a scrawny girl trapped in her desolate hospital bed. Her tiny paralyzed body was swallowed by her hospital gown and blanket as she watched the world pass her by, unable to talk, unable to move. I never thought she would make it out of that bed, much less that she would be talking and walking. She opened my eyes to the strength of love and the human spirit. I do not know how circumstances led to us meeting each other three years ago, when I was a nervous, new volunteer, or how we came to reunite on my last day of playing guitar at the hospital. But I do know that we both needed each other in our lives at these times. Perhaps serendipity should not be interrogated, but rather appreciated.

***

After leaving Laney's room, I felt inexpressibly grateful for the last three years of opportunities to share my talents and my heart with sick children at the hospital. It was overwhelming to think back on all the patients I had encountered, those living as well as those who passed on. They had let me into their lives, and they showed me that I can always do something to help heal the world, however small the act. In the face of cancer, epilepsy and death, I plucked the strings on my beat-up guitar and sang songs. By no means did I save lives, but I did do my part. And the reward was a collection of memories that will help to sustain me for the rest of my life.

At the end of the day, I slowly packed my guitar into its ragged case and prepared to leave the floor for the last time. I tucked away my guitar, maracas, capo and song binder, but there was still room left in the case, so I began to load in the memories of patients from the past three years. I added Laney with her "thumbs ups", Joey and his buffalo, a teenage boy with a freshly amputated leg, a bald-headed girl asking me if I was a doctor or a musician, a six year old boy who had just relapsed again, an 8 year old boy with a brand new heart, a Jamaican family who wanted to sing a song about three little birds, knowing that every little thing was gonna be alright. I loaded the smiling and crying faces from every child I had met with my guitar in hand, and I loaded the many lessons they had taught me. Then I carefully closed the case and slung it over my shoulder, ready to carry these memories into the next chapter of my life.

Acknowledgments

This book would not have been possible without the support of many people and institutions. I am very grateful to the Cleveland Clinic Children's Hospital and the Department of Child Life Specialists, especially Tom Richards, for allowing me to volunteer at the hospital. Additionally, I am grateful to my medical school, Cleveland Clinic Lerner College of Medicine, for encouraging and supporting the medical humanities in the medical school curriculum. Also, Dr. Kathy Franco was a great supporter of my idea to play guitar for children in the hospital, and she has been a continual source of encouragement as I develop my career as a physician and writer. Lastly, I owe many thanks to my colleagues who read various drafts and offered valuable insights. In particular, Kay Sisk, Jennifer Madsen, Maryanna Lanning, Dr. Richard Prayson, Maj Ragain, Jim Lang, Dr. Kathy Franco, Adam Skaggs, Rachel Norton, Dr. Jim Young and Dr. Lisa Middleton all helped in this regard.

ABOUT THE AUTHOR

BRYAN SISK is a medical student at the Cleveland Clinic Lerner College of Medicine of Case Western Reserve University. His undergraduate training was in biochemistry at the University of Missouri—Columbia. He is an avid musician and writer, and has volunteered his talents in the pediatric hospital by playing music for sick children and their families. He is currently pursuing a career in academic pediatric medicine. He can be reached at ALastingEffect@gmail.com.

8783678R0

Made in the USA
Charleston, SC
14 July 2011